Left by t

Story o. ___

MW01601536

Left by the Indians:

Story of My Life

ETHAN E. HARRIS

Other books by Ethan E. Harris:

The Gospel According to Joseph Smith
Custer Survivors 101
The Bare Bones List

As Editor:

Reno Vindicated
Stop Them Now

Preface

I have always been fascinated by stories of endurance and tales of survivors of significant historical events. A few years ago, I discovered that my wife's ancestors included the Fanno and Van Ornum families. Both of those families had immigrated to Oregon by way of the Oregon Trail in the mid-1800s. During that trip, many members of the Van Ornum family fell victim to a lengthy, cross-country assault on their wagon train. This book is the eyewitness story experienced by a girl on the wagon train and their eventual rescue.

Ethan E. Harris

ORIGINAL PREFACE

It is at the request of many friends I consent to publish the story of my life. They have heard enough of what I have suffered by the Indians, to make them anxious to hear or read the rest. To repeat the whole story to every individual that wants to hear it is an impossibility — hence I write that they may read for themselves. In preparing it, I have sought only to relate the narrative in language that the children can understand without difficulty. It is not for money that I write (although whatever may come to me by means of the following pages, will be very acceptable) but rather to accommodate my kind friends and neighbors, and to lead all who may chance to read it in to deeper sympathy for the suffering members of the human family.

Its mission is therefore to create sympathy and bring the blessings of mercy to the unfortunate. If this is accomplished even on a small scale, I shall feel abundantly rewarded for any trouble I have taken to send it out on its little mission.

The portraits of the deceased have been transferred from the only ones I have of them. They are not quite satisfactory. The artist in Chicago did the best he could with them but owing to the dimness of the old tintypes from which they were taken, he could not present a good picture. But I thought that they would answer a purpose. I trust, therefore, that all who read will look kindly on all defects. I extend sincere thanks to all who have assisted me in any way in preparing this little pamphlet for the public.

Mrs. Emeline L. Fuller
Marshfield, WI

INTRODUCTION

The story of the life of Emeline L. Fuller of Marshfield, Wisconsin.

We happened to be called to that city by the M. E. Church of which she is a member, to hold a tabernacle meeting last summer, and hence became acquainted with Mrs. Fuller. She attended our meetings regularly over two weeks before we knew that her life was so eventful.

Often, we noticed her careworn face and listened to her solemn testimony and heard her weighty words on an important church affair. All meant something to us. We noticed also that she did not kneel when she came to the altar. She was deprived of this luxury as well may others by previous suffering. But being invited to dine at her home with others, part of her history was placed in my hand, and I read with profound interest. I mentioned it at the dinner table, and she broke down in tears, and told us the whole story.

We then learned all we could from every source concerning her life. We obtained some valuable information from her uncle Jason Payne with whom we had the pleasure of dining while in the city. But a letter that she sent back to Wisconsin shortly after the fight, which contained some things that we would all like fight, which contained some things that we would all like to read was lost, or it would be given in substance in this little book. We were deeply affected by hearing the story, and meeting with one who had suffered so much at the hands of the Indians.

We never expected to meet with one who had such a terrible experience to tell.

When we had gathered all the information we could on the subject, we requested her to commit it to our care that it might be published, and after some deliberation she consented to do so. And now, dear reader, as you read for yourself, I trust that this narrative will melt your heart into deeper sympathy with the suffering and innocently unfortunate members of human society, as it did mine.

Yours Truly,
James Hughes
Mt. Vernon, Iowa
24 DEC 1891

STORY OF MY LIFE

My father was born in Mt. Vernon, Ohio in 1824 and my mother was born in Gelena, Wisconsin on July 12th, 1827. Her maiden name was Abagel Payne. They were married January 1st, 1846, at Sugar Creek Walworth County, Wis. To them were born three children, of whom I was the oldest. Christopher was born November 28th, 1850. He was always vigorous and full of fun. Libbie was born January 9th, 1852. She was always a delicate child, and hence a great care to me.

I was born Feb. 21st, 1847 at Mercellon, Columbia County, Wis. When I was five years old we moved to Keokuk County, Iowa. We traveled with oxen and wagon. When all was in readiness to start as we supposed, father noticed that he had not fixed a place to carry a pail with which to water the oxen on the way. He took a nail and while driving it in a crosspiece under the wagon, the nail flew and struck my right eye as I was looking on, causing almost total loss of vision ever since.

We arrived at uncle William Trimble's after a journey of over two weeks. Father rented a house for us and went to work at whatever he could get to do. In the fall of 1852 father being away with a threshing machine, was called home on account of mother's sickness. She had the Typhoid fever. Soon after she recovered father took the same disease and died. After father's death Uncle George Trimble came after mother and us children, and took us back to Walworth County, Wis. where we remained for a year. The next spring we went to Winnebago County, to my grandfather Payne's and stayed till the fall. Then we went to my mother's brother, Uriah Payne. He was a widower, with three children. My mother kept house for him till the following spring.

Here I wish to mention a little incident that occurred, because of what follows. I loved my little brother Christy dearly. One day mother hid the axe from him for fear he might cut himself, but I found it and gave it to him. Soon after I was passing where he was chopping and accidentally fell, and my left hand went under the axe as it came down and I lost my large finger for finding the axe, Children do suffer for not minding their parents. But poor Christy felt worse about it than I did. He cried as though his heart would break, and we could not get him to come in the house till late that night.

From there we moved to Fondulac County, near Brandon, and remained about a year and a half. Then we moved back to Columbia County to my uncle Jason Payne's, and remained, till spring. From here my Uncle Geo. Trimble's son took us back to Walworth County, where we helped to care for grandfather and grandmother.

1

In 1858, mother married Elijah Utter, of Walworth County, a blacksmith by occupation, and a large-hearted, honest man, who proved a good husband to mother, and good father to us children. He had three sons and three daughters, making in all eleven in the family. The next year a baby daughter was born to them, making twelve in the family.

My father and mother often talked of going to the far west to make themselves a home, and settle their numerous family in homes adjoining their own in that broad country, where settlers were so much needed to till the lands, and improve the country, and after much deliberation and very much advice from friends and neighbors, they decided to go, and commenced preparations forthwith, selling their home and converting other property into money, buying oxen and wagons, and preparing for our long journey, for we had decided that we would go to Oregon, which was full six months journey in our way of travel. I could but contrast the old ways of travel with the new, as I made the journey a short time ago in six days, comfortably seated in a police car. The first day of May, 1860, dawned upon us clear and bright, and with all prepared for starting, we yoked our oxen to the wagons, gathered our cows and young stock together, taking sixteen head and four yoke of oxen, our family dog, clothing, provisions, household utensils, and although tears were in our eyes at the thought of parting with our friends and relatives, still we were hopeful, for we dearly loved each other, stepfather, stepbrothers and sisters all being united and happy, and the thought that in that far land to which we were to go, we would be so fortunate as to live an unbroken family in nice homes, near father and mother, and if the Lord so willed it, with not a face missing in our family circle, gave strength to pass through the sorrowful parting. But I shall never forget the tearful faces of my dear old grandparents as they stood at the end of the lane, leading to the road, with tears streaming down their wrinkled faces bid a last adieu to their youngest child and her family.

The Wagon Train

I was then a girl of 13 years, and with a heart untouched by cares, but bitterly did I cry over leaving home, and lonely, most lonely were the first few nights of camping, and feeling that we were going farther and farther from home each day.

We fell in with three other teams about noon of the first day that like ourselves were started for Oregon and California. As these families were with us during our entire journey, I will give their names: John Myers, who left his wife and children and went to find a home for them, Michael Myers, a brother, and Edward Prine. With this addition to our company we felt a little stronger and better satisfied. We soon became accustomed to camp life and after a little time really enjoyed it.

Everything had been planned before starting on our journey, and we had prepared all things for convenience on the road. We took ten milk cows, and had kegs made before starting, and we milked our cows and strained the milk into our kegs, put them into our wagons, and every night the milk was churned by the motion of the wagons into nice butter, which we salted and worked into balls for use.

We stopped and rested our teams occasionally and did our washing and such work as it was possible to do up ahead under the circumstances.

We kept falling in with emigrant teams, and by the time we had reached Ft. Laramie we had quite a train.

There are many incidents of our journey which I should like to narrate if time and space would allow. One young man by the name of John Green, who overtook us at Ft. Laramie, while handling his revolver, had the misfortune to get his hand shot, and so badly hurt that he had to go to Ft. Kearney and have it amputated.

We were much amused by the intelligence and acuteness of the little prairie dogs. Some nights we scarcely slept at all for the barking and yelping of the noisy things, which alarmed at having strange neighbors and wished to alarm their friends. They had little owls and a kind of dormant rattlesnake in the burrough with them all on friendly terms, it seemed. We stopped at Fort Laramie a few days to rest and shoe our teams, also to wait for teams which we heard were behind us, and like ourselves bound for Oregon. We fell in with a large California train, and traveled with them until the Californian trail separated from the Oregon, and then we were left more lonely than before. We had felt the security of traveling with such a large number. While with the Californian train, when we camped at night we would prepare the ground by cutting down the brush, leveling and sprinkling the ground, and have a good old-fashioned dance.

It was not much work to make our toilets, for the most of us wore for convenience the costume called Bloomers and did not have many changes. We would also sing songs, tell stories, and amuse ourselves with all the sports of our school days, feeling perfectly safe and secure, for in union was our strength, but how soon all changed when we parted with our friends of the California train, and traveled westward, knowing that we were every day nearing the dangerous part of our journey. But still we kept on over hills, through forests, across mountains and rivers, until we came to Ft. Hall, where soldiers were stationed. As we deemed it unsafe to go farther alone, we called for troops to go with us. There had one company already gone with a train but a few days ahead of us, and we had to wait for the soldiers to make preparations.

While waiting, Col. Howe, in command of Ft. Hall, sent in a request to have the women and girls of the train come into their tents and have a dance, which we refused to do, which very much displeased the Col., and at first he refused to send one of his men with us, but upon considering the matter over he dared not refuse, so sent out a small force, with instructions not to go more than half as far with us as those he sent with the train ahead. The soldiers, when they turned back, told us that we were just in the edge of danger, and so we found it. For in a few days we found the Indians meant mischief, as they did not come to our wagons, but would occasionally come in sight at a distance, seemed to be watching us, and acted as though they were not friendly to us. One of the soldiers deserted and went with us. He was a bugler, and took his bugle with him, but we did not enjoy music as well as when we felt safer.

After we had traveled for about one week, perhaps longer, we camped late one night. We had not been in camp long when three Indians and two squaws came into camp and all agreed that the leader among them must be a white man, as his dress and appearance was different from the rest. He had a beard, and you could see plainly that he was painted. He wore an old white hat, with the top of the crown gone.

We could tell him as far as we could see him; he was so different from the rest. They stayed around our wagons until late, when our men told them that they must go to their homes, as we wish to go to bed. They waited to be told a number of times, and finally went away.

We started early next morning and did not go far before we came to good feed and water, and as we had a dry camp the night before, the men decided to stop part of the day and water and feed the teams and stock, and let the women wash. In a short time, the same Indians came to us, talked a while, and told us they were going off into the mountains to hunt, said good bye, and left us. We were suspicious of them, and the men consulted together, and thought the safest way would be to kill them, but hardly dared to do so, for fear of its being found out by the Indians. Still we all thought them spies, and I often wish that we had done as our better judgment told us, and killed them and secreted the bodies, but it seemed it was not to be so. All went well for a week.

We saw no Indians to alarm us, and had almost regained our cheerfulness, and were very hopeful that our fears were unfounded, when on reaching Salmon Falls, on Snake River, who should we meet but our supposed white man and the two Indians who were with him before, and a number of other Indians with them. They came to our wagons and pretended to be glad to see us. We bought some dried salmon of them, and hurried away, thankful to be rid of them, but it worried us as we were followed. We went on for another week with all quiet, and we were another hundred miles nearer our destination, when we reached a small river, I think it was called Bruno. There we found a good place for our stock to graze. We always sent a man out with the cattle and horses, for fear they would be stolen, and when our cattle were brought into camp at night there were one or two yoke of oxen missing. The men searched for them and found their tracks where they had been driven up a canyon by Indians.

We kept a good watch that night and were not molested. In the morning Mr. Van Ornum, the man who lost the oxen, threw away everything that he could spare, and someone let him have a yoke of oxen to hitch to his wagon, and we all started along feeling glad to leave what seemed to us to be a dangerous place. We traveled only a short distance before we came to a grave where a man belonging to the train ahead of us had been buried, and the Indians had dug him up, taken his clothing, and then partly buried him, leaving one hand and foot out of the grave. You cannot imagine what a terror struck to our hearts as we gazed on the awful sight and reflected that we too might share the same fate, for on looking about us we saw a board on which was written an account of his being killed by the Indians, and warning anyone who came that way to be very cautious. But the warning came too late to do good, for we had not gone more than a mile before we were attacked by them.

The Attack

This was the 9th day of September 1860. As we came up the hill and turned down towards Snake River again, we came in full sight of the Indians who were singing their war songs, and their shrill war whoop I can never forget. It was too terrible to even attempt to describe but suffice it to say that although so many years have elapsed since that awful, awful scene, I can never hear a shrill yell without shrinking with much the feelings which I experienced as that terrible noise reached our ears.

We saw at a glance what we must do and corralled our wagons as quickly as possible. There were only nine wagons in the train, but we had sixteen men and boys capable of bearing arms and were well armed. There were also five women, and twenty-one children between the ages of one and fourteen years. Perhaps it might be of interest to tell you of the families in the train: Elijah Utter and wife, with their ten children, Mr. and Mrs. Myers, with five children, Mr. and Mrs. Van Ornum, and five children.

After a short time, the Chief rode up and down the road waving a white cloth and motioning for us to go on at noon. Two or three of the Indians came up close to us and motioned that they wished to talk with us. Some of the men went out and met them, and they said they would not hurt us, that they were only hungry, and that we were to go on after noon, but I can tell you that dinner time did not find us with our accustomed appetites that day.

Shortly after noon we started but did not go by the road as they expected us to do, but kept up the hill from them, and the last wagon had hardly started before they commenced their terrible war songs and dancing again and coming toward us all the time. We corralled our wagons as soon as possible, but before we could get the last one in place, the man who was driving was shot dead. His name was Lewis Lawson, from Iowa. Shortly after two more were killed, Mr. Utley and Mr. Kithual. We fought them all that afternoon all of that long, awful night, picking them off as often as we could get a chance. We had no chance to get away under cover of night, as they were watchful, and if they heard the least noise would commence whooping and shooting at us. We talked it over and made up our minds that we were all to die but thought we would try leaving all the wagons but one for each family, and take some provisions, leave all our stock and other property, and see if they would not let us go our way. There were with us three discharged soldiers from Fort Hall, and the deserter before mentioned. They were mounted on horses and were to go ahead and clear the way for us to follow with our wagons. But instead of doing so, the discharged soldiers put spurs to the horses, which belonged to Mr. Van Ornum, and galloped off for dear life, and left us to our fate. The deserter stayed as long as he could and stand any chance to save himself, and then taking with him the Reath brothers, Joseph and Jacob, they left, taking the one horse with them which belonged to the deserter. In the horrible tumult of the light we did not see them go and did not know but they were killed.

The Indians now seemed to redouble their frenzy and showered upon us a continual fire, until it seemed impossible for one to escape. The first one who fell there was John Myers, who it will be remembered left his family at home either at Hebron, Illinois or Geneva, Wisconsin. As Joseph Reath was helping my oldest step-sister, Mary Utter, from his wagon, a ball passed through his clothes and entered her breast. She only lived a few minutes. The next one to go was my step-father, who had his baby, one year old that day, in his arms. As I stepped up and took her from him, so he could the better use his gun, I kissed him and turned to mother, who was bending over my dying step-sister, Mary, when father was shot in the breast and fell. He got up, but hardly got up when he fell close to his daughter Mary, and soon died. We gave up then. It seemed as though our whole dependence had been taken from us, and leaving our wagons, we started, each one for himself. I turned to my poor mother who was standing by the dead bodies of husband and children, and begged her to go with us, but she said no, there was no use in trying that we were all to be killed, and that she could not leave father, and when I found that I could not persuade her to go, I took one last lingering look at her dear face, and taking my poor little baby sister in my arms and telling four of the little brothers and sisters to follow me. I started, I knew not whither, but with the one hope of getting away from the wretches who seemed to thirst for the blood of every one of us. I turned and motioned to my mother, who still stood by the wagon where I left her, with two of my step-sisters and a little step-brother. She shook her head, but the oldest step-sister started to come to me and they shot her down. I turned and ran a little way, and looked back, and they had all been shot down, and were lying with the rest of the dead. I felt then that all that I held dear on earth was dependent upon my feeble care, and child as I was, I nerved myself for that terrible struggle for life which I could see was before me.

Will the reader of this narrative please to pause a moment and reflect upon my situation? A child of barely thirteen years, and slender in build and constitution, taking a nursing babe of one year, and four other children, all younger than herself, and fleeing for life without provisions and barely clothing enough to cover us, into the pathless wilderness or

7

what is worse yet, across the barren plains of the west. It was now the 10th day of Sept., and getting dark, the second day after the attack. Others also fled, and we got together as much as possible and made for the river, for we were very thirsty, as we had had but little water through the night, for we did not fill our kegs as usual that morning, as we knew we should travel along the river. After we got a drink of water we rested a little, if it could be called resting, with the awful fear in our minds that we should be followed and killed. We decided upon the course that we would keep away from the road and travel in single file, and as near as possible cover our tracks by having a man step in each track.

We traveled by night and hid in the willows that grew along the river, by day. We traveled only a short distance that night and we could see the fire from our burning wagons and such goods as they could not well carry away, and before morning we hid in the willows on the river bank and lay there all day. We saw some of the Indians going past us driving off some of our cattle, for it seemed that they divided up into small bands and dividing their spoil, each one went his way. While they were passing I held my hand over the mouth of my baby sister, who, frightened, perhaps by the scared faces around her commenced crying. Poor little sister, how my heart did ache for her. Words cannot describe my agony as I looked on the faces of my little brothers and sisters, poor orphans now, and heard them cry piteously for father and mother, and if possible worse yet, cry for bread when I had none to give them. God grant that none of the readers of this story may ever realize from experience the awful bitterness of the cup which I was forced to drink to the very dregs.

Just about dark of that day three Indians went past us shooting off their guns and whooping and yelling. We laid very quiet until after dark, then got up and traveled as fast as possible. When tired out we would lie down and sleep a short time, then get up and travel along.

The Indians followed us four days, coming onto us about the same hour each night. We supposed they tracked us all day. The fourth night they did not come until later. We had camped under a hill on the creek, and above us were rocks, and they went up above us and rolled rocks down, trying to roll them onto us. They came close, but we were so far under that they did not strike us. We started as soon as it was dark enough for us to travel with safety, and kept on all night, feeling sure that we would be safer elsewhere. One night, brother Christopher was missing when we camped. You will remember that we traveled by moonlight and starlight, and we could not guess what had become of him, and one of the men went back and found that he had taken the road and gone on, instead of turning out where we did to camp. He found his tracks, but we did not see him until the next day, when we met him coming back to us.

After the fourth day we did not see nor hear anything to alarm us and traveled by day and camped by night.

You will perhaps wonder what we could get to eat. Well, we got so hungry during the third night's travel that we killed our faithful family dog, that had shared our hardships through all that long journey. We also killed Mr. Van Ornum's, roasted and ate some of the meat, and carried the rest along for future use.

We kept on our journey through the wilderness until we came to the Owyhee River, near where Fort Boise used to stand, and all being tired out with travel and weak with hunger, we camped there.

We had found a cow the day before, which had strayed away from the train ahead of us and was trying to go back home. She was very poor, but we shot her, the first shot which had been fired since we left the wagons. We roasted her and carried the meat over to the Owyhee.

We had traveled more than 100 miles, although it would not have been much over 80 by the road, since leaving the wagons, but so far all were alive, although our sufferings were terrible, both from hunger and exposure. It was getting cold weather, and we were without extra clothing nights, and commenced to suffer from the cold. Our shoes were worn off, and we were barefoot, or nearly so, and nights we would bury our poor bruised feet in the sand to keep them warm. We set to work and built us camps out of the boughs and brush which we could find along the river, for we could see little probability of getting away from there and tried to make things as comfortable as possible. Mr. Myers had escaped so far with his whole family, and had it not been for him I think we should have traveled along a little way each day toward the Fort, which was to us the haven of safety, but he begged so piteously for us not to leave him, as he was not able to travel, that we would not go without him.

When we had been in camp some time, my brother Christopher was down by the river fishing one day, when an Indian came to him and seemed much surprised at seeing him and wanted him to go home to his camp with him, but Christy told him that he had a camp of his own and must go to that. He went away, and Christy came home and told us. In about an hour the same Indian came back and had four more with him, and brought us one fish, but when they saw how many there were of us, they went back and brought some more fish for us, and urged us to go to their camp with them, but we would not go. We had a great horror of being taken captive by them. We traded some of our clothes with them for fish, and they wanted Christy to go home with them, and he told us that he would go home with them, as he was afraid that if none of us went, they would not like it, and might do us harm. He was a brave little fellow, and although only eleven years of age, had before started with a man by the name of Goodsel to see if they could not reach the fort and bring us help, and after getting quite a long way from us they met the deserted soldier and the Reath boys, who got away, it will be remembered, at the time of the massacre, taking one horse among them, and in trying to reach the fort they had taken wrong road, and brother and Mr. Goodsel met them coming back to take the right trail. When they heard that we were starving they killed their horse and roasted it and started my brother back to us with all he could carry, and he, poor boy, knowing how great was our need, loaded himself so heavy that he had to throw pieces away as it became so heavy that he could not carry it. The man Goodsel went on with them, traveling with all speed to reach the fort and send help to us.

But to return to my subject, Christy said that if the Indians did not let him come back that he could run away the next summer and get in with some emigrant train and reach us if we ever got through, which looked very doubtful. The Indians took a dislike to the children of Mr. Van Ornum, as they were so hungry that they snatched the fish from them and ate it greedily.

They went back to camp taking Christy with them and said they would be back in three days and bring him with them. After they went away, we talked it over and thought when the back, me back they would surely kill us, and Mr. Van Ornum and wife, with two sons and three daughters, Mr. Gleason and Charles and Henry Utter, my step-brothers started along to try and reach Walla Walla.

At the end of three days the Indians came back as they had agreed to, and brought Christy with them, and they brought fish again. Mr. Chase ate so much of it that he was taken with the hiccough and died. We buried him, but the Indians dug him up, took his clothes, and buried him again. My poor sister Libbie, nine years old, used to help me gather buffalo chips for fuel, and rosebuds, pusley and other things to eat. She and I went to gather fuel as usual one morning, and she was tugging along with all she could carry and fell behind. I carried mine into camp and went back to meet her. I called her by name and she made no answer. Soon, I found her, and I said, "Libbie, why did you not answer?" She said, "I could not talk I felt too bad," and before night she was dead. Soon the Indians came again bringing Christy with them. I did not see him this time as I was away after fuel. Mr. Myers asked him where they camped. Christy asked why he wished to know, and he said, "because when the soldiers come we want to come and get you." The Indians, as soon as they heard the word "soldiers" spoken, said it over to each other and talked among themselves and went away taking Christy with them again. I came back with my fuel, and when on my way out quite a ways from camp I heard a frightful noise. It seemed to me more like dogs fighting than anything else I ever heard. I was scared, and made haste into camp, and they told me Christy had been there and gone back again. We waited with as much anxiety as we could feel about anything until the three days were passed back, the Indians did not come back, and we felt afraid of them, and we began to talk about trying to start along, but I could not go without finding something of the fate of Christy.

We waited a few days and then I went over to Snake River, about two miles, and I could see their camps, but could not see any living thing around them. I called Christy loud and long, but the echo of my own voice was all the answer I could hear. I went back to camp feeling sure that something had happened to the boy. The next day Mr. Myers took the trail which went from our camp to theirs and had not gone far when he found where the wolves had dragged something along, and soon he found some of his hair, and then he knew that my brother had been killed by the Indians and his body torn to pieces by the wolves. He came back to camp and told us, and words cannot describe my feelings as I heard of his horrible fate. I knew then that the noise which I heard that day was my poor brave Christy whom I loved so well. I thought I had passed through all the suffering which I could endure. And God knows how I longed to lie down and die and be at rest, but it was not to be so, nor had I drained the cup to the dregs yet. Starvation was making sad inroads on our little band, and none but those who endured the awful pangs of starvation can have even a faint idea of such horrible sufferings and death. We became almost frantic. Food we must have, but how should we get it? Then an idea took possession of our minds which we could not even mention to each other, so horrid, so revolting to even think of but the awful madness of hunger was upon us, and we cooked and ate the bodies of each of the poor children, first sister Libbie, then Mr. Chase's little boys, and next my darling little baby sister, whom I had carried in my arms through all that long dreary journey and slept with hugged to my heart, as though if possible I would shield her from all danger. She too had to leave me. In vain had I saved the choicest morsel of everything for her, chewed fish and fed it to her, boiled pusley which we found on Snake river, and fed her the water, and everything which I could plan had been fed to her to keep her alive.

11

Mrs. Myers and Mrs. Chase each had babies about her age, but neither could spare a share of nature's food for our poor little motherless one, for fear of robbing her own. For over forty days I had carried her, but had to give her up at last, and I was left alone. All who had depended upon me had been taken away except the two step-brothers, who had gone on and from whom we had heard nothing. We also dug up the body of Mr. Chase, intending to eat that, but thank God, relief came. The first one to reach Fort Walla Walla was one of discharged soldiers, who it will be remembered, ran away with Mr. Van Ornum's horses from the wagons at the time of the massacre. They told so many lies on getting to the fort, that the soldiers did not believe that there was any train in trouble. He got in a number of days before the Reath brothers, Mr. Goodsel and the deserted soldier gave out on the way and did not reach Fort Walla Walla. They camped there till the soldiers came after us.

When they reached the fort, which was between eighty and a hundred miles from us, one of the Reath boys came back with two companies of soldiers, one of dragoons and one of infantry. They started back immediately and traveled along without resting night or day.

Rescued

Upon nearing us, they found a sad sight. The company who had gone on ahead when the Indians took brother Christy away, which you will remember consisted of Mr. and Mrs. Van Ornum, three daughters and two sons, Samuel Gleason, and Charles and Henry Utter, the Indians had followed and killed Mr. and Mrs. Van Ornum, their son Mark Samuel Gleason, and the last of our family except myself, Charles and Henry Utter. Their bodies lay unburied, showing marks of torture too devilish for any human beings to inflict except Indians. Let those who have never suffered as I have pity the fate of the noble red man of the forest. My pity all goes out for their poor unfortunate victims, and I can never look even upon one of our poor, degraded, harmless Winnebago's without such feelings as I do not like to entertain towards any of God's created beings, and I almost doubt if they are a part of our great Maker's work.

Mrs. Van Ornum had evidently been tortured too terribly to mention. Her ankles were tied with strong ropes when found, and she had been scalped. Three of the Van Ornum girls and one boy had been carried away by the Indians. The next year we heard, by some emigrant trains, something of them. The oldest girl, 13 years old, was killed. In attempting to get away she killed two squaws, and the Indians then killed her. The boy was bought by an emigrant train and reached his uncle in Oregon. The Indians were seen leading the two little girls with collars around their necks, and chains to them to lead them by. A thousand pities that they had not all been killed with their parents. I have that one consolation, that in all my troubles none of my folks were taken captive by them.

The dragoons commenced to bury the dead, who it was very evident had been dead but a short time but the Heath boy begged of them not to stop there for the night, as it was getting late in the afternoon, but to push on for he told them there were certainly more somewhere, and it was possible they might find them alive. So, the infantry traveled all night without resting. I may say here there is no doubt, but we owed our lives to that night's work of those brave, tender-hearted men, for we were sure that the Indians were on their way to kill us when scared away by the approach of soldiers.

About ten o'clock in the morning we saw signal fires off a few miles from our camp, and we knew that either they were coming to kill us, or help was close at hand, and strange as it may seem to my readers my heart was so benumbed by my terrible sufferings that I hardly cared which it was. I was alone in the world and had suffered enough in the past few months to change me from a light-hearted child into a broken-hearted woman, and my wish was that I might lie down and die and join my kindred in a world free from cares and troubles like those I had passed through. I was out after fuel as usual, when I saw the soldiers coming, but was too weak to feel much joy at seeing them. They rode up to me and a few dismounted and coming to me asked if I did not want something to eat. I answered that I did not care. I shall never forget the pitying looks bent on me by those strong men. Tears stood in every eye as one of the officers gave me a part of a biscuit. I ate that, but did not care for more, but in a few days, I was hungry enough to eat anything. I could not have lived many days longer if help had not reached us.

The soldiers commenced at once making preparations for return to the fort. They took us about three miles from our camp the next day after their arrival, and went into camp there, and waited for us to get ready. They told us to make us some clothing before starting. We made some skirts out of blankets which they gave us, and we wore some of their underclothes, and their short blue coats, which were comfortable, for it was getting to be cold days and nights, as it was now the 25th or 20th of October. I cannot speak half well enough of the soldiers to express their kind and gentlemanly treatment of us, and I shall carry through life the recollection not only of the kindness but even of the features of those large-hearted soldiers, and I almost think I should recognize any of them, should I ever see them. They made saddle-bags, hung them across their saddles, and put a child in each one: made a litter for those who were too feeble to ride on horseback, or rather on mules, for they were mounted on mules. Mrs. Chase and myself changed, and each rode a part of the time on a litter. I have neglected to say that Mrs. Chase had the misfortune to lose the use of one limb, and the arm on the same side, and was almost entirely helpless, for a part of the time we were in camp, and it was very hard for her to travel in any other way than on a litter. She got thrown oft' from the mule and hurt, and then I gave up my place on the litter to her. After traveling a few days, the government wagons sent to our relief from Fort Walla Walla met us. Then we had clothes to keep us warm, and an easy wagon to ride in.

Perhaps some of my readers will wonder why we ventured so much danger with so small a train. The reason is we did not intend to cross those dangerous plains alone. We fully expected to overtake a train that was a short distance ahead which got through all right except the one man above mentioned, who left the train to go after some strayed sheep and was then killed by the Indians. Having failed to overtake them, we were left to our sad fate in spite of all we could do.

14

There was one family which I cannot forbear to make special mention of, and that is the family of Mr. Myers. The reader will recollect that I spoke of them in the beginning of this narrative. There were seven in the family, father, mother, and five children, and strange as it may seem every one of them were spared and reached the fort in safety. Mr. Myers, in answer to the question asked him how they all happened to get through, when other families were entirely annihilated, answered. "It was prayer saved my family," but I can say that my idea is that extreme selfishness had more to do with their being saved than prayer. The hardship of gathering fuel and subsistence was not shared by Mr. Myers' family. He said they were not able. Even the task of washing for their baby was allotted to me, and often when we would go out after pusley, rosebuds, and such other vegetation as we could find, which we could eat, and leave Mr. Myers praying. I suppose in a selfish way, for his own family, in camp, instead of helping in our hardships, on our return the other children would cry and beg for something to eat and say the Myers family had been eating fish, or whatever we had stored away for rations, for we had to allow each one just so much at a meal. Perhaps the good Lord, who is the searcher of all hearts, heeded his selfish prayers, but I would quicker believe that shirking duty and stealing from others was what saved the Myers family.

Moving On

After I arrived at Walla Walla, Washington Territory, I stayed with the family of Lieutenant A. J. Anderson until my cousin came for me from Salem, Oregon. It was the Lieutenant that rescued us at Owyhee River near old Fort Boise. They were very kind to me. Mrs. Chase and her little girl stayed at the home of Captain Dent. He was a brother-in-law of U. S. Grant, and captain of the infantry. They were there when I left.

It was now about the middle of December 1860. My cousin took me to his sister's, who had married Mr. T. J. Pomeroy. My cousin's father, Edward Trimble, was killed on the plains in 1846 by the Indians. From Salem I went to Linn County, Oregon, to my only relatives in Oregon that I had ever seen before, Uncle Pierce Trimble and his family moved to Oregon in 1853 from Walworth County, Wisconsin. With them I made my home part of the time, and part of the time with Mr. W. W. Allingham's family, and went to school. They were very kind people; in fact, all I met with in the west were kind to me and often tried to help me to forget my troubles. I shall always hold in grateful remembrance the kindness of the people in Washington Territory and Oregon. They were so liberal in making up money for us. My uncle took what was raised for me and bought sheep with it for me. I had twenty-one head. Uncle gave me a cow, and Mr. John Clark gave me another. So, I had plenty of stock.

My schooling did not cost me nor my uncle one cent, as the people paid for it. Neither did their kindness stop here. They often came and took me along to entertainments that were going on in the country. The best horse and saddle were always provided for me. They wanted me to learn to ride on horseback, as that was their mode of traveling there. I soon learned to ride, and often went with the young people to church and singing school. Sometimes eight or ten couple of us went together. The country was beautiful to ride over, and the scenery was lovely to look at. When the snow was three or four feet deep in Wisconsin, I picked wild flowers in Oregon. Everything around me, so far as nature was concerned, was charming to behold. If father, mother, brothers, and sisters had only been with me, my joy would have been complete; but they were gone, and with all that beauty spread before me, I could not help but turn my longing heart toward them, and weep in my loneliness. While in the schoolroom trying hard to learn, the scenes of the past would come up before me, and it seemed that my heart would break. Nobody knew how hard it was. Many times, I was happy with my young friends, and tried to be so; but night would come on, and I would pray for dear mother to come and take me and cry myself to sleep. My feet were so injured from walking after the fight, having no shoes, and from the cold, I could not always walk to school. Then I rode on horseback and picketed my horse out till I returned home. I still suffer much pain in my feet.

I lived in Linn County about two years, and then went forty miles to Monmouth, Polk County, Oregon, with a lady I had met a few times. She had me go to the Christian College in that place. I went two terms, and then came back to Linn County in the spring. The next fall (Nov. 12th, 1863), Mr. John M. Whitman and I were united in marriage. Mr. Whitman was born September 8th, at Monmouth, Ill. When he was eight years old his parents moved to Monmouth, Oregon, taking him along. His parents still live there. Here we began house-keeping and remained till the following July. During this time, I received a letter from my mother's uncle, Rev. Aaron Payne of Yamhill County, Oregon. His brother was a Quaker preacher and Blackhawk's first victim. They captured him on the way to his appointment. He carried no arms, according to the Quaker custom. The Indians said he was a brave man to travel there in this way; but even this heroic spirit did not prevent them from taking his defenseless head and carrying it on a pole. Rev. A. Payne had been a widower since 1847. His family had all died with the consumption, except one son. He wanted me to come and live with them. He came twice to see me before I was married, and if possible to get me to go and live with a family near them and go to school. The first time he came he talked to my uncle, but did not mention it to me, lest I should become uneasy. Uncle did not want me to go.

After we were married we went and lived on his place two years, and he lived with us. Then we moved to Tillamook County on the coast, about fifty miles distant, to another place of his, taking with us some of his stock with our own. We took a preemption joining his place for ourselves and got along well. Every turn we made seemed to be in the right direction, for we made money fast, and were happy. We lived in that part five years. To get there we had to cross the Coast Range of mountains on horseback or go around on the water. We usually preferred to cross the mountains. Those mountains are covered with the finest timber that can be found. The timber in Wisconsin looks like shrubbery beside those great trees. The fruit was abundant and delicious. The climate was very mild. They hardly ever had snow to lie long enough to have a sleigh-ride. It is a great place for fishing and boating. We used to have some good times with our neighbors, sailing and rowing. Three or four couples of us often went to the beach and camped all night. Some would take their bathing-suits along and go out in the water as the tide came in, and let the waves roll over them. We often walked miles on the beach, dug clams, gathered shells, etc., to pass the time away, and amuse ourselves. When we got tired we would return to our campfire and sing songs and visit to make life as pleasant as possible. It was amusing to see some strangers trying to go out with a boat on the tide. Not being aware that the water was so shallow, they sometimes neglected till the tide left them on a clam-bed or mudflat. There they might play themselves for six hours, until the tide would return and bring them back. As I looked on those majestic mountains, the dark, briny ocean, and the blue, ethereal sky; I thought of Him, who made the mountains rise;

"That spread the flowing seas abroad and built the lofty skies."

In 1870 we sold the property we had there and went to Eastern Oregon. The damp winter seasons did not agree with my poor health in the west. Here we rented a good farm from a brother-in-law for two seasons and did well. We raised feed and bought and sold stock. Then we moved about one hundred and thirty miles into Washington Territory. Here we took a homestead timber claim and bought some railroad land adjoining. We farmed, kept a store and stage stand, or traveler's home. Many of the officers and soldiers of the late war stopped with us; Generals Howard and Wheaton I remember well. I shall never forget the thrill that went through my heart when I saw Gen. Howard's empty sleeve. He was the first officer, or soldier, that I had seen who lost a limb in the war. I thought of my own cousins and friends, who had been killed or wounded fighting for the same cause. After the death of my husband our property there was sold and passed into the hands of strangers, and now there is a city on our old place. I should like to see it once more. While residing there we adopted a nephew of my husband. He was eleven years old and lived with us till he was twenty-one. Now he is married and settled in Rosalia, Wash.

Since I returned to Wisconsin, Mr. Melvin Fuller of Pardeeville, Wis., and I were married. He was a widower with seven children at home. We lived together for four years and a few months and then separated on account of trouble with the older children. Now I live beside my uncle Payne, and his family in Marshfield, Wis., and Miss Nettie Reid stays with me most of the time. In 1861 I was converted to God and joined the Close Communion Baptist church. Since then I have found Jesus to be a "friend that sticketh closer than a brother."

In 1873 we took Frank Riggs to raise. He was only six years old. His mother was from Wisconsin. She went to Idaho to keep house for her brother, Joe Raker. She married Mr. Riggs and in a few years, he left her and the children to the mercy of strangers in Western Oregon. If any of her folks should happen to read this, I should like very much to hear from them. But before this when we were in Eastern Oregon we took his baby brother only two weeks old. Their mother having four children. Baby Willie (as we called him) grew to be a sweet and good little fellow but he was permitted to stay with us only six years and seven months. He died Aug. 22, 1879. It was hard to give him up, but God knows best. I shall meet my dear ones some sweet day in that beautiful heaven beyond.

Far from a world of grief and sin,
With God eternally,
Emeline L. Fuller

Made in the USA
Las Vegas, NV
21 August 2021